KT-364-035

The Happy Recruiter
The 7 Ways to Succeed

By James Reed

1 3 5 7 9 10 8 6 4 2

Published in 2019 by Virgin Books, an imprint of Ebury Publishing,
20 Vauxhall Bridge Road,
London SW1V 2SA

Virgin Books is part of the Penguin Random House group
of companies whose addresses can be found at
global.penguinrandomhouse.com

Penguin
Random House
UK

Text Copyright © James Reed 2019
Illustrations © Rosie Reed 2019

James Reed has asserted his right to be identified as the author of this Work in
accordance with the Copyright, Designs and Patents Act 1988

First published by Virgin Books in 2019

www.penguin.co.uk

A CIP catalogue record for this book is available from the British Library

ISBN 9780753554166

Typeset in 12/16 pt Bembo Std
by Integra Software Services Pvt. Ltd, Pondicherry

Printed and bound in Great Britain by Clays Ltd, Elcograf S.p.A.

MIX
Paper from
responsible sources
FSC® C018179

Penguin Random House is committed to a sustainable
future for our business, our readers and our planet.
This book is made from Forest Stewardship Council®
certified paper.

For my father

'Above all, I believe that a sense of humour is vital.'
Sir Alec Reed

Contents

What Makes a Successful Recruitment Consultant?

When I was a teenager, back in the last century, I applied for a local holiday job through a recruitment agency and to my delight was offered a clerical placement at the princely rate of £2.50 an hour. My first morning went well, but at lunchtime I was surprised to see everyone packing up to go home. It turned out that the company only operated during the mornings, a somewhat important fact my recruitment consultant had neglected to tell me. After mentally downgrading my earnings to half of what I'd been expecting, I decided there must be a better way for recruiters to manage things.

Fast forward to today, and I'm the Chairman and Chief Executive of REED, Britain's best-known recruitment brand and the employer of a network of over 2,000 recruitment professionals. I've spent the past 25 years working with countless recruiters from both REED and elsewhere, and having thousands of conversations about all things recruitment-related. I'm also happy to admit that getting things right in recruitment isn't as easy as I thought it was when I had my first job.

I've always been fascinated by what makes one recruiter successful and another not. It's no secret that recruitment is a 'Marmite' profession – people seem to either love it or hate it. Like baby turtles headed for the sea, only the most determined newly hatched consultants will survive and thrive long term. And even when they've been in the job for a few years there are further pitfalls to avoid. Are you aware, for instance, of two of the worst mistakes a recruiter can make? The first is to request references from a candidate's current employer, landing that candidate in the soup with their boss. The second is to ruin their own reputation by failing to pay their temporary workers promptly on a Friday, revealing poor financial management in the process.

So what do you have to do, or be, to become a successful recruitment consultant? This is the million–dollar question, and being able to answer it (or, even better, personify it) leads to rich rewards. When you perform at a high level, you can both transform your candidates' lives for the better and enhance the effectiveness of your clients' organisations. This requires a deep understanding of human nature, a commercial awareness of how businesses are run, and the ability to delight players on both sides of the recruitment equation continuously and consistently. It sounds like a tall order – and it is – but you can give your chances of success a significant boost by actioning the insights and advice in this book.

I've been travelling around the country having conversations with recruiters for a quarter of a century – conversations that have formed the basis of this book. I also crowdsourced advice from my network of thousands of recruiter customers, asking them: 'If you could go back to "you" on the first day of your recruitment career and give yourself one piece of advice, what would it be?' I received some revealing answers, which included the importance of specialising, the central role played by strong relationships, and why being both resilient and time-urgent are key. These weren't the only areas I was interested in, though. By researching my recruiter base I also discovered new tips for keeping up-to-date with the market, ways of working quickly but without sacrificing quality, and tricks for persevering when it feels as if the world's against you.

I was pleased to discover that recruitment is widely regarded as a rewarding career. Most of the people I canvassed had worked in the field for over ten years, and 85 per cent were satisfied or highly satisfied with their jobs. One of our top consultants, a woman in her late twenties who used to work part-time in her mother's hair salon, now earns a six-figure sum and is one of the best recruiters in the country. She doesn't have a degree or many years of experience, but she loves people and is incredibly good at working with them.

The crowdsourced insights I gained make up the lessons in this book and you'll see quotes, included at regular intervals throughout, from the recruiters with whom I spent time. This is to keep the advice authentic. There's nothing worse than reading a lot of theory that you can't see working in practice, which is why this guide is short, sweet and based firmly in the real world.

The Happy
Recruiter

EAST SUSSEX COUNTY COUNCIL
WITHDRAWN
10 JUN 2024

17

04641626

How to use this book

To be a happy recruiter, I think that you should possess seven key attributes, or personas, that you can adopt throughout your career. You won't use them all at the same time because they're flexible and can be drawn upon to suit your needs, but you should be aware of them so you can employ them in different circumstances. I've called them the 'Seven Rs', and together they make up the cogs in a happy recruiter's engine. You're about to learn what they are, why they're important and how to develop them for yourself.

To bring the Seven Rs to life, I've assigned to each of them a 'spirit animal' that you can summon in times of need. Why a spirit animal? Well, I've observed over the years that success in recruitment requires spirit, and the animals I've chosen encapsulate the different types of spirit that take the successful recruiter forward. An eccentricity? Perhaps, but it works for me. I've explained why I've chosen these creatures within the relevant attribute below – see if you can relate to them as you read about them.

So, who are the different types of recruiter you should be capable of being? They are:

The relatable recruiter, who builds relationships that foster trust. This recruiter is as likeable and communal as a **dolphin** as it mingles with the others in its pod. A dolphin is never on its own but thrives on communicating closely with its 'colleagues', and as a result makes up an indispensable part of its group.

The relevant recruiter, who knows their field inside out. For this recruiter's spirit animal I've chosen what might at first seem an odd choice – an **anteater**. In the same way as the relevant recruiter is particular about what specialism they work with, an anteater will predominantly eat one type of food and has adapted itself perfectly to the purpose.

The ready recruiter, who's prepared for any eventuality. Like a **spider** that's woven its web ready to snag a passing fly, a ready recruiter must invest in planning how to use the opportunities that come their way. Then, when the time is right, their steadfast work will pay off.

The rapid recruiter, who's quick enough to win the best candidate or client. This recruiter is as speedy and nimble as a **hare**, darting through the undergrowth at a moment's notice. You don't always see it until it pops up in exactly the right place at the right time, barely breaking a sweat. Speed is in its nature.

The resilient recruiter, who keeps going no matter what. Just like a **tortoise**, in fact. Both recruiter and tortoise are steadfast and patient, with this creature having the added advantage of a ready-made, protective shell. When obstacles present themselves, the resilient recruiter works around them and moves on.

The reflective recruiter, who never stops learning. I like to compare this kind of recruiter to an **owl** because insight and discernment are priceless. As far back as Greek mythological times, the owl's large eyes and serious face have symbolised wisdom, and many believed that the bird had an inner light that let them see at night. The reflective recruiter has a similar hidden advantage, because self-knowledge is power.

All of these qualities lead to . . .

. . . the rewarded recruiter, who's fulfilled and respected for every aspect of their work. They can be compared to a **bee** in its hive, reaping the rewards of hard work. A hive buzzes with activity and never stops, producing delicious golden honey as the payback for the bee's efforts.

As you go through this list, ask yourself: do these recruiters and animals sound like me? And if not, could I learn to be a little more like them? Could I get in touch with my inner dolphin?

Think of this book as the professional recruiter's bible – only shorter. You should find that individual chapters will match your current circumstances. For instance, if you're finding it hard to win over a client, try the 'Relatable' chapter, and if you've had a bad week and aren't sure how to motivate yourself, the 'Resilient' chapter is a good place to go. Ultimately you'll become a 'Rewarded' recruiter – enhancing the lives of your candidates and clients, taking home a sizeable pay cheque and finding enrichment for yourself along the way.

I hope you enjoy the journey.

Chapter 1
The Relatable Recruiter

There's no doubt about it, recruitment is a people business. You spend a lot of your time on the phone or meeting clients and candidates in person, so being a relatable recruiter is the most important kind you can be. In fact, when I asked one of my longest-serving recruiters which of the seven Rs they would focus on the most, they replied, 'Relatability, relatability, relatability.' The spirit animal I've chosen to symbolise relatability is the dolphin, because of how closely it interacts with its pod. In the same way, being relatable for a recruiter is about helping people to feel a sense of connection with you so they trust you to put their best interests at heart.

I have a client who I first placed as a candidate 28 years ago. I've placed her four times and now her daughter five. Today, both of them are clients and give their business to me.

– Specialist Recruiter

In a way, you're not unlike a matchmaker in that your role is to introduce one stranger to another. Much of your work should therefore be centred on taking away the 'stranger' element by creating consistent and rewarding partnerships with both your clients and candidates. This involves building lasting relationships through being warm, open and easy to talk to. Along with this comes trust, because all enduring relationships are built on it – the ability to generate trust is fundamental to being a relatable recruiter.

In our personal lives, developing a relationship with someone isn't something we always do deliberately. We simply find that when we get on with someone and enjoy spending time with them, we've somehow become friends. But when you're a recruiter, you need to be more intentional with forming connections, as this chapter will show.

How to be relatable

We all know recruiters who have the gift of the gab, but does it help them to build relationships that last? As the word suggests, being relatable is about *relationships*, not one-off sales. Here are the best ways to be a relatable recruiter, gleaned from my many conversations with recruitment professionals.

Be a people pleaser

Many recruiters are what can be described as 'people pleasers', which comes in handy when you're in a job that's based on keeping two external parties happy. It can sometimes seem like an impossible task, but pleasing people essentially comes down to treating others as you would like to be treated yourself. When you care deeply about satisfying their needs, you'll find your desk plays host to an endless parade of quality matches, and you'll feel motivated from the core to provide an exceptional service.

With clients especially, this involves seeing them as more than a pay cheque. When you know what hobbies they have, where they go on holiday and what they think of their new boss, you show you care. As time goes by, you'll become increasingly engaged with them and they with

Providing excellent customer service to both clients and candidates is key, as without either we wouldn't have a business. My clients and candidates keep coming back to me because I know them and their business – what they need and what they don't like.

– Recruitment Manager

you, which makes your relationship easier to manage than if it's only surface deep. For instance, you'll find they trust you to do their candidate CV screening, and they'll take your calls readily because they know you always have something useful to say. You'll also have fun working with each other and earn more from them in the long term, because they want to do repeat business with you.

Think about how you interact with people at all levels of your client organisations. When you visit a company, it's essential to treat the receptionist with as much respect as you would their manager, not only because it's good manners but because that same manager will often ask the receptionist what they thought of you as soon as you've left. If you treat the gatekeeper as an irrelevance, you can kiss that important relationship goodbye.

It's the small things that count, such as learning and using people's names. Making sure everyone you speak with remembers you in a positive way right from the beginning, asking yourself how you'd feel if you were them and treating people as individuals are all building blocks in the pursuit of good relationships. And never forget the power of a 'thank you' for a client – you can express this through a simple phone call, a letter or card, or a random act of kindness such as sending them a box of chocolates to make them the most popular person in the office that day.

I want to find people jobs because I feel that that is what I should do for them. I want to fill temporary bookings quickly, because I feel that is what my client needs. My desire to demonstrate my 'good' makes sure I deliver speedily and efficiently.

– Senior Consultant

Be honest

Being honest should be easy, but we all know this isn't necessarily the case. Have you ever felt bamboozled by a client's job description, or pressured into saying you'll deliver eight quality candidates by tomorrow when you know you only have four? It takes courage to say, 'Sorry, can you explain what you mean? I don't understand,' or 'I know you'd love more candidates but I honestly think the four I have will be enough for your needs.' Worrying about looking stupid is always misplaced – everyone appreciates it when you come clean.

Ask any candidate what their worst experience of a recruiter has been and they'll probably tell you it was the recruiter promising the earth when it wasn't in their power to give it. This usually comes down to the consultant wanting to help the candidate, but it's easy to see how it can backfire. If you're open with your candidates they'll be more likely to be upfront with you, so when you ask them if they're working with any other agencies, for instance, they'll tell you the truth. This can be a huge help when you're marketing the candidates to clients.

The same goes for when you're making promises to your clients. By all means give yourself a tight deadline but make sure you can stick to it, otherwise you'll disappoint

Be honest and don't sell a lie just to make a fee . . . it will always come back to bite you!

– Recruitment Consultant

them and lose their trust (not to mention denting the reputation of yourself, your organisation and your profession). Apart from anything else, it just makes sense. When you're realistic with both parties it decreases the chances of candidates dropping out or of clients turning them down, both major timewasters in our field. This also applies when you're negotiating salaries. Close your clients low and your candidates high. For instance, if a candidate will accept a salary of £30,000 and the client will pay up to £35,000, agree the placement at £33,000 and everyone's happy.

Being honest about something that you can't deliver can involve having tricky conversations, and it's best to do this upfront so it's not eating away at you. As Mark Twain once said, 'If it's your job to eat a frog it's best to do it first thing in the morning. And if it's your job to eat two frogs, it's best to eat the biggest one first.' Just get on with it before worrying about it has taken up your whole day.

Finally, never is it more important to be honest than when you've made a dreaded mistake (this happens to us all). It may seem like a good idea to cover up your blunder, but letting someone down is only the second worst thing you can do to them. The absolute worst is to lose their confidence and trust, because that can be impossible to win back. It's amazing how few people will come clean in difficult situations, so handling things

> The 'unicorn' candidate doesn't always exist. When I consult with a client I use the 5-3-1 strategy. From the job description I ask them to tell me five requirements that they would like, three that they want, and one that they absolutely need.

– Recruitment Consultant

honestly and constructively can go a long way towards neutralising the effects of your error.

Take your time

It's natural to want to sign up a new client or place a candidate in a matter of days (and who doesn't love the adrenaline rush when that happens?), but the reality is that, like Rome, relationships have never been built in a day. Striking a careful balance between following up with clients on a regular basis and not overwhelming them with phone calls is the best way to go. How do you know what that balance should be? Ask them what level of contact they would find helpful.

When it comes to filling a placement, rushing to shortlist candidates who aren't a good fit for your client's organisation is never a good idea, because it erodes the trust they have in you. You need to be patient and a good listener – really hear what they're after and have the tenacity to follow it up methodically.

Turn up

Did you know that if you secure a face-to-face meeting with a client to discuss a job and the lead time, you're four times more likely to fill the role than if you do it over the phone? There's something about the phone that makes you more easily forgotten, whereas if you take the

Often candidates have long notice periods for finance. It may take up to three to six months for the entire hiring process, so you need to build relationships with these people.

– Specialist Recruiter

It's important to meet your clients and visit their site. It's really helpful in marketing the job to the candidate. You can tell them things that they wouldn't know from the job spec alone. Things like: what is the team like? What's the culture like? What's the commute time?

– Recruitment Consultant

trouble to pay a personal visit you have the chance to build rapport and get to know them on a deeper level — people buy from those they know. If you're struggling to persuade your client to agree to you taking the job details in person, try this: 'You rightly expect me to have met all the candidates I send you and, in the same way, they expect me to have met you before I recommend them for the job.'

Why not book a day out of your diary once every couple of weeks to visit six or eight clients? If you have 30 active ones, that means you'll see each of them once a quarter. They'll appreciate you giving them a market update, salary survey or even just a hello, and will often raise an issue or ask a question that they wouldn't have thought about over the phone or email. The reassurance they'll gain from this could make the difference between them coming to you for their next placement and searching elsewhere. While you're in their area, you could also drop in on a few prospects — that business park with 20 offices could be a fertile ground for new customers. Just don't make the same mistake that one of our recruiters did. In a bid to develop relationships with local hiring managers, he rang all the ones he had on his database for a particular company. He asked if they would like a personal delivery of a desk diary for the new year, to which many said yes. On the allotted day he turned up but couldn't find any of the people to whom he'd spoken. It turned out that they were all based in a different city miles away, which meant he had to sheepishly call them up to explain why they hadn't received their diaries.

How's this for a tip? When you have a large client you've been trying to speak to for months but who won't agree to a visit from you, and you have a temporary worker already placed with them, pay the temp a visit and bring a gift. Make a bit of a fuss in the office when you give it to them and ensure there's some branding on it. Other temps may look enviously at the recipient and contact you later to register with you. There's no need to be invited in through the front door – sometimes the back one will do.

You can also create opportunities for meeting both existing and prospective clients by organising events for them. These could be social, such as taking them out to lunch, or professional, such as employment law seminars or industry update talks. You can ask a local specialist firm to provide a presentation and host it on your premises, with everyone having the chance to network and learn. It's a great way of finding out what your clients are most interested in and positioning yourself as a helpful, go-to recruiter at the same time.

Be yourself

Sometimes it can feel as if all you do is sell, sell, sell, and when that happens you know you're going off track. Of course, recruitment involves marketing your agency and jobs to candidates, but try not to see each call as a pitch or you'll come across as robotic and self-serving. People buy from people and in your case that means from *you*, not anyone else. So be yourself on a call – in fact, it's one of your strongest competitive advantages because no one can be you as well as . . . well . . . you.

This goes both ways. Sometimes you'll find yourself dealing with a potential client who you find objectionable or unpleasant. Remember, it's your decision who you work with, and if you don't think you can get on with that person, you don't have to progress the relationship. Running a recruitment desk is a bit like managing your own business – you have a choice who you trade with. When you love your clients you'll give your all to them, but if you ignore your preferences just to make a sale, the cracks in the relationship will start to show. Knowing and being yourself also has another benefit, which is that you're likely to trust your judgement when something doesn't feel right instead of ignoring it for the sake of putting across the correct image.

No sales pitches, I just share information clearly and correctly between both parties.

– Recruitment Consultant

Don't forget your candidates

Recruiters are naturally empathetic towards their candidates, which is more than can be said for some clients. One recruiter I met told me that they'd had a candidate who'd failed to turn up for an interview because they'd just been rushed to hospital. 'What a shame,' said the client when they were informed. 'Can you reschedule them for tomorrow?'

Joking aside, the number-one reason why many clients are reluctant to use a recruitment agency is because they once had a bad experience of that same agency as a candidate. As the maxim goes, 'Never forget that today's candidate is tomorrow's client.' Apart from anything else, it makes sense to look after your candidates because you've gone to the trouble of interviewing and registering them, so why would you want them to feel tempted to look elsewhere? They're also more likely to perform well at interview if they feel confident that you're on their side.

What do candidates value? One of their main gripes is that recruiters are all over them like a rash when they have a suitable role for them to fill, but that once the job is gone they're dropped like a stone. Job seekers also want feedback when they're not successful at interview, and even when they are. Think of the effort they've gone

I've had seven years out of the profession and I still get people coming to me, which is testament to the relationships I've built with candidates.

– Specialist Recruiter

to in researching the company, turning up to be grilled and performing in a nerve-wracking situation – they don't want it to be for nothing. So while you're focusing on retaining your clients, pay equal attention to your candidates. Why not give them a call to see how their job search is going and ask if there's anything you can do to help? Many of my recruiters have a whiteboard on which they write the types of roles for which they're recruiting. They aim to have at least five pre-existing candidates underneath each one, and call them every week. How happy you keep your candidates should be as much a measure of your success as how well you retain your clients.

Also, understand what a candidate's motivators are. They may want a pay rise but that's probably not all – it's your job to discover their deepest need. Is it a better work–life balance? A shorter commute? A more interesting challenge? When you know what they're after, you're in a better position to deliver it to them, and they'll thank you for it. You have to be excited by your candidates because you need to sell them to your client – if you don't know them well enough to relate to them, you can't do that effectively.

One thing you can be sure about with candidates is that they're great at spreading the word among themselves. The first question they'll be asked by their colleagues when

If the client doesn't give feedback, you could have a role-play interview with the candidate to see where they're going wrong.

– Specialist Recruiter

they hand in their notice is, 'How did you land the job?' If the answer is 'X at Recruitment Consultancy Y — they were excellent', you can be sure this will lead to a queue of new job seekers at your door without you having to do any legwork. You have a significant chance to make a name for yourself when you're recommended like this.

Be relatable even when you don't feel like it

Recruitment is a job in which you have to be spirited to do well — people need to like you. At the same time, we all have off days and there are times when your patience will be tested to the limit. One of the most frustrating elements of your job can be the unpredictability of people. No matter how many times you ask a candidate what other roles they're applying for, they won't always be straight with you, and clients are notorious for ignoring phone messages or not keeping you in the loop when they have a change in recruitment strategy.

This is where the quality of your professional relationships comes into its own. When candidates trust you to act in their best interests they'll be more likely to give you the full picture of their job search, and when clients value your opinion they'll be more inclined to be honest with you. It's a virtuous circle. Relatability is the key to being happy in recruitment even when it seems like an uphill struggle.

It can sound easy, just matching a candidate with a client, but sometimes there are a lot of external factors that you have to manage, as well as dealing with everyone's expectations. It's challenging.

– Senior Executive Consultant

To sum up

- Treat clients and candidates as you would like to be treated yourself (and remember that today's job seeker is tomorrow's client). It sounds simple, and it is.

- Be honest and upfront with people and it will pay dividends, even if it's not always comfortable at the time.

- Getting to know people takes time, so spend it on the right people, and remember that nothing can replace the effectiveness of a face-to-face meeting.

- Don't forget to be yourself – you're not a salesperson, you're **you**.

- It's not always easy to be relatable, but the better you get on with people the more naturally it comes over time.

Chapter 2
The Relevant Recruiter

Have you ever heard of the singer Chesney Hawkes? In 1991 he released a huge hit that topped the UK singles chart and reached the top ten in the United States, but after that he never had the same success again. The song was called, ironically, 'The One and Only'. I'm guessing you don't want to be a one-hit wonder like Chesney either, but that's how you might end up if you don't build a depth of knowledge in your specialist area.

Just like our spirit animal friend the anteater, whose long nose is designed for hoovering up ants from the tops of anthills without harming their home, the relevant recruiter is a specialist who is perfectly adapted to their environment.

Today, we live in an age of expertise. Recruitment, whether temporary or permanent, is no exception to this, and there are many recruiters who limit themselves to what at first glance might seem to be narrow fields such as accountancy practice, cyber security, digital marketing or further education. This is a smart move because your clients expect you to know as much about their world as they do. How else are you to judge whether or not a particular candidate fits the bill? Being able to speak your client's language is vital for your credibility, as well as being a cornerstone of your reputation as a knowledgeable and helpful recruiter. In fact, when anyone asks me what I do for a living and I answer 'recruitment', their next question is always, 'What do you specialise in?' What they're really asking is, 'Can you help me?' or 'Can you relate to what I do?' In a profession where human connections are fundamental, what you specialise in is part and parcel of your success.

Becoming an expert is essential for carving out a reputation, as everyone will be impressed when they see you have in-depth knowledge. It also helps you to narrow down your client and candidate search, because you'll be focusing on the specialist media they read and the groups they attend. You'll also find it much easier to market your candidates when you're confident that they know their stuff.

Ten years ago I could survive on personality and rapport-building. I can't do that now, you need that and specialist expertise.

– Area Manager

There's another element to being relevant, which is to do with tailoring your approach to people. We all have our preferences and inclinations, and like them to be taken into account. In this chapter I'll not only cover how to become an expert in your recruitment field, but also how to talk to your contacts in the way that works best for them. By the end, you'll be the ultimate relevant recruiter.

How to be relevant

The truth is, anyone can become an expert in pretty much anything if they want. Sources of knowledge are like watering holes – they're freely available, so you just need to know where they are and keep drinking from them every day. Even when you're up to speed and can recite by heart the main issues, challenges and facts relating to your industry, you should keep returning to the watering holes to refresh your knowledge and make sure you are 'the recruiter who knows everything about . . . '

Become knowledgeable and stay that way

First of all, be clear about your specialism. What kind of expert do you want to be, not only in terms of your area but also the subsection within it? For instance, if you specialise in accountancy, what kind? Big city firms? Boutique practices? Accountants for specific industries? You may not find yourself working in your niche full time, but it's a huge selling point for you if you have one because you can be the go-to recruiter for it. And you'll know all the key players, which makes it a lot easier to pick up the phone to the right person. However, it may take time at first to find the special corner of your sector you're most interested in, so be prepared to keep an open mind at first.

The best recruiters have more in common with the people they're recruiting than they do with other recruiters.

– Specialist Recruiter

There are many ways to learn about the industry and sector you're recruiting in. An obvious place to start is online, where resources are quick and easy to access, but as well as Googling your specialism, it can be worth signing up for blogs and newsletters to drip-feed knowledge into your brain. You can also glean a lot from the websites of your clients and their competitors, of course, including the language they use, the areas of interest and the hot topics that are top-of-mind for them. Social platforms are another rich resource. See if you can join relevant LinkedIn and Facebook groups, and follow thought leaders on Twitter. These will give you a special insight into the controversies and personalities that predominate, as well as potentially introducing you to new clients and candidates. Naturally, if your client base is active on some other social network, sign up to that instead.

Your next port of call is to talk with your candidates. If you're at the beginning of your specialist journey, go out and meet as many as you can. Rather than only treating the interview as a tick-box exercise for a job, ask open questions about their field and don't pretend you know more than you do. Your aim is to understand what an average day looks like for them and what they see as the main factors in their career success. Once you've spoken with a couple, you can use what you learned to ask more developed questions of the next, and so on. The less

When I was recruiting for manufacturing roles, I had a manufacturing weekly newsletter delivered to my inbox and read it. This enabled me to have informed conversations with clients about the sector.

– Specialist Recruiter

talking you do, and the more listening, the better – show a genuine interest.

Your clients also represent an opportunity to learn more, and most people love being asked for advice. Make it your goal never to have a phone call with a client that doesn't help you dig out some piece of insider information about their marketplace. Next time you pay a personal visit, pick up their company brochure and check out the magazines they have in their waiting area – these are all sources of information about their sector.

Finally, don't forget your colleagues. There may be others in your agency who have been working in your sector for years, and there's a lot you can absorb by chatting with them and hearing what they have to say. Some recruitment agencies have a weekly meeting at which everyone is expected to bring some market intelligence – this not only helps you to learn, but also gives you an added incentive to keep up-to-date because you won't want to be underqualified. And what about specialist seminars and update lunches? Their main aim is to foster client relationships, but you can also use them as a way of gaining market insight for yourself.

You can always stay relevant by reading the news, but the absolute best way to stay relevant is to ask questions of your candidates and clients all the time.

– Area Manager

Enjoy your expertise

You'll find it easier to learn and keep up-to-date if you enjoy your niche – it will feel like a hobby to discover more and more each day. You need to be genuinely fascinated by it. What makes it tick? What challenges does it face? What's helping it to grow?

If you don't have an affinity for your specialism, your job will feel like hard work. Think of the candidates you're placing – you can't market the job to them if you're not able to relate to why they want to work there. If you find you're not enjoying your niche, though, all is not lost. You might be happier working in a different division of your agency, or even a new one altogether. This is an area where it really is important to be selective.

Use your relevance to boost your sales

Once you've become a true expert, make the most of it. Ensure you bring nuggets of information to your client and candidate conversations, use the right buzzwords and demonstrate that you're aware of the latest developments. If your sector is education, for instance, you'll want to show an understanding of the budget constraints schools are under and how important it is for a new teacher to be able to work independently from day one. Your specialist knowledge then becomes part of your unique selling point as a recruiter, and allows you to

Even within retail there are different specialisms: fashion, luxury and so on. We need to make sure that anyone going in knows exactly what they're talking about, because otherwise down the road it'll become apparent to the candidates you're speaking to and also to the clients.

– Recruitment Consultant

Share relevant news with your clients. If you have little knowledge of their marketplace and sector, you aren't talking the same language.

– Senior Business Manager

ask the right questions of your candidates. You can also use your insight to anticipate when your clients will need to recruit more staff, because you'll be on top of their cyclical employment patterns and any unexpected disruptions in their industry. That way you'll be 'in there' before anyone else is.

Being relevant is a great way of building trusting relationships, but once you've done that you need to take what you know about a particular role and relate that to your industry. Attending conferences is a fantastic way to learn more about your field and tap into a pool of candidates you wouldn't have met otherwise. An additional income stream for you, if your agency is run like this, is to split fees with other specialists by networking internally – if your expertise isn't right for a candidate, you can pass them to someone more suitable.

Alongside this, bear in mind that being a trusted specialist may mean turning down a client on occasion. If their mission doesn't match yours, how well can you serve them? And what would it mean to your personal brand if the best recruiter for interim lawyers turned out to have a sideline in the beauty industry? Clients talk to each other, so don't let the messages you send out confuse them. You will risk losing their trust.

In my experience if you fail to persuade somebody it is usually because somewhere along the sales cycle you have forgotten to make your pitch relevant.

– Senior Area Manager

Tailor your talk

An often-overlooked aspect of being a relevant recruiter is the importance of flexing your approach to the client or candidate in question. Naturally, one of the ways you can do this is by showcasing your expertise as it relates to the role, but there are others too.

Tailoring your behaviour to your client, even down to what you wear, helps to create rapport. For instance, a corporate lawyer wouldn't appreciate you bouncing in and being too casual because they'd expect a reserved approach, whereas a tech start-up might be surprised if you were overly formal. Be super alert to the circumstances you find yourself in so that you stand out in the right way.

Another way to flex your approach is to ensure that you listen actively to what your client wants, and shortlist according to their needs. This seems obvious but it can be easy to forget in the daily pressure of reaching your targets, tempting you to bombard clients with CVs just to make up the numbers. You can also keep an eye out for any awards your clients have won and congratulate them when you next speak – a little flattery never goes amiss. And finally, be a hoarder of useful facts. If you can remember what you learned from client conversations, such as the promotion they were going for, or the project that was causing them stress, you win brownie points.

My ex-girlfriend used to be horrified that she'd say something and I'd remember it months later, but as a recruiter the smallest thing that you can remember from a client conversation is like gold dust.

– Talent Acquisition Manager

You can also be relevant when it comes to searching for candidates in the first place. For a start, make sure you're using the most appropriate channels to find them. This will obviously include your own client database, which you can mine using targeted search techniques, but also social media, job boards and CV libraries, external events, your colleagues and even your local jobcentre (which will book you a day to screen people if you ask). I call these channels the 'one per-centers', because although they may yield small numbers each time, if you make use of them every day you can double your results in a year.

Once you've pulled together a shortlist of candidates for a role, it's important to screen them by phone before you arrange a full interview. The reason for this is – you guessed it – to ensure they're relevant for the job. Questions you'll want to ask include whether they have any restrictions on working in the country, any background issues such as criminal convictions that could cause a problem, and if they have a disability that would affect where you interview them in person. This means that, once you come to the full interview, you know you're only talking to people who are eligible for the job.

To sum up

- *Use online resources, clients, candidates and colleagues to become informed about your specialist area and to stay that way.*

- *Discover a specialism that you enjoy and feel interested in, otherwise you'll find it hard to be enthusiastic about it.*

- *The purpose of being relevant is to increase your sales, so use it in your client and candidate conversations.*

- *Another way of being relevant is to tailor your conversations and search techniques to specific client and candidate needs.*

- *Make sure you're seen as relevant in your language and appearance, both on- and offline.*

Chapter 3
The Ready Recruiter

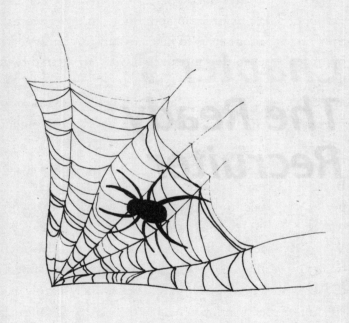

The most successful recruiters approach their work as a footballer does a penalty shoot-out – with practice, organisation and vision. In other words, they prepare themselves to take advantage of every opportunity, even the unexpected ones. You could be just like your spirit animal, the spider, which can produce as much as seven types of thread, each serving a distinct purpose: you set yourself up for success through proactive and consistent efforts ahead of time.

Being ready has twin advantages: you're in a great position to make the most of anything that comes your way, and you're less likely to panic if problems arise. When your newest client asks you to fill five placements by next month, you already have the job seekers lined up to suit. And when your biggest client cancels a role at the last minute yet again, you're able to offer your candidates an alternative interview instead.

This means being organised, and one of the best things about this is that not only will you be able to cope with the ups and downs of your job, but you'll also save time and create efficiency in your working day. Make sure you have a plan, because having a plan makes you proactive. Being in the habit of thinking ahead makes your work easy to manage, especially in a people-centred business such as recruitment, where both candidates and clients can change their minds at will. What's more, the readier you are, the more you'll be seen as someone who can be relied upon whatever the circumstances. Having a recruitment consultant who takes everything in their stride and delivers top results consistently is a huge relief to a frazzled HR manager or panicking job seeker. Never underestimate the value of being a safe port in a storm.

How to be ready

The process of recruiting is so much easier when you realise that's what it is: a *process*. You can have all the panache you like on the phone, but if you don't have a way of organising yourself you'll become lost in a maze of unanswered calls, forgotten leads and missed opportunities. Emergencies happen and the unexpected will always arise, but when you're operating from a place of order and calm these problems are relatively easy to deal with because you're not trying to juggle too many tasks at once. With that in mind, this chapter gives you some solid and practical tips for systematising your work so that you're fully prepared for any eventuality.

Be like a soldier

Some people are naturally organised, but even the most efficient of us could do with some help in this area. Having a set way of doing things also helps to prevent embarrassing mistakes. One recruiter with whom I spoke confessed she'd had a candidate at final stage interview for a job in a valuable client's business and, while this was in progress, had registered another candidate who worked for that same company. So far so good, but because she hadn't kept accurate records she mistakenly specced the new candidate to a number of

companies he'd expressed an interest in, including . . .
the organisation he already worked for. The recruiter
returned from lunch to an outraged email from her
client, who informed her that their professional
relationship was over. And no, the original candidate
didn't get the job.

This shows the value of writing everything down. Also,
don't be afraid to ask questions so that you have all the
facts to hand — there's nothing more likely to create
a stressful emergency than realising you don't know
whether a client requires a specific qualification for a
role, or if there's parking at their office.

Do one thing at a time. You might like to think you can
multitask like some kind of superhero, but the reality is
you're only human — too many jobs left half-finished
leads to chaos. You can always spot the disorganised
recruiter from the litter of Post-it notes, half-eaten
sandwiches and CVs on their desk — it's obvious that they
haven't taken full ownership of their role. The armed
forces are a great role model for this. Someone once told
me that when you join the army there are three simple
rules you must stick to every day: shower morning and
evening, wear deodorant and put on a clean shirt.

Rules that create consistency in how you spend your
time are helpful. How about blocking out parts of your

Don't die wondering, just ask the questions.

– Recruitment Consultant

week for certain tasks? For instance, you could make business development calls between 9am and 12pm, and prospective candidate calls between 8am and 9am, 12pm and 1pm, and 5pm and 7pm (when they're less likely to be at work). Also, set aside slots for registrations, visits and meetings. Some weeks you'll find your routine going out of the window, and that's fine because you need to build in enough flexibility to respond to unexpected opportunities, but at least you'll be ensuring the basics are done each week.

Once you've set up your overall routine, you need a way of carrying out your regular activities that works for you. For instance, do you have a process for what you do once you've sent CVs to clients? How about creating a template email or two that you can adapt to go along with them, and deciding a set time for you to wait before you follow up? There's no need to be rigid about it – all clients will have their preferences – but if you know what you plan to do upfront it's clear for everyone.

Be consistent

Clients love consistency, and the recruitment consultants who get to know their clients over time will build trusting relationships with them. If you want a company to think of you first, you need to keep nurturing that relationship, otherwise you'll find that six months down

We created a process for when we sent CVs across, saying, ' . . . three suitable CVs are attached. We've also attached further candidates who may not have all the skills you're looking for, but having met them we think they'd be worth a look.' What that does is guarantee the top three will all get interviews.

– Area Manager

the line they've called the agent that did keep in touch. If you're keen to work with them, show it by making regular contact.

At any one time your client list will be split into three groups: core clients (the ones you have retainers with or have worked with for years), active clients (the others you currently work with) and target clients (the companies you want to work with in future). It's tempting to assume that your core clients are 'in the bag', but this isn't necessarily the case — they can leave at any time. So make sure you speak with them, on the phone or in person, at least once a week and do the same with your actives if possible. As for your target clients, they should number 20 or 30 at most. Qualifying who they are is essential because they should be businesses with whom you can reasonably expect to place candidates. You'll invest time in developing them, so watch out for those who are lovely to chat with but who will never use your services. You might be surprised that your target client list should be so small, but bear in mind that you're wanting to know them as *people* and you can't do that if you're chasing too many at once. A concerted effort focused on a few is more productive than a hit-and-miss series of calls to 100.

If you genuinely care about your clients, doing what you said you were going to do comes easily. Once you've made a placement you'll find yourself wanting to check that all is well — in fact, the hardest thing to do can be to leave them alone so they have some breathing space. Agreeing a system upfront is helpful here, for instance that you'll contact them within six weeks of the candidate starting and follow up three months later for a more in-depth chat.

Candidates love consistency too, which should come in the form of feedback on your progress and on their interview performance. Let them know if they've impressed the hiring manager for a job they've been interviewed for and keep them in the loop about what you're doing for them. Every time.

Be ready to make an impact on your clients and prospects

Becoming a client's favourite recruiter doesn't happen by accident — it's the result of meticulous preparation. Don't be like an embarrassed consultant I once met who'd just delivered a huge marketing pitch. He rounded it off with a triumphant, 'We really want to work with you,' at which point the client asked him, 'So what do you know about our business?' The consultant had no idea about the company to whom he was talking and, needless to say, was shown the door.

I had a candidate the other day who asked, 'What are you doing for me?' and I told him that I'd sent an e-shot to 135 managers and out of those 24 had got back to me to say that they were interested. So let people know what you're doing and keep in contact throughout.

– Specialist Consultant

Having a structured approach isn't just helpful for your overall process: it can also be invaluable for every marketing call and conversation you have. Did you know that in the UK, a medium-sized business receives 180 sales calls a week on average? If you haven't considered how yours is going to stand out, you'll struggle to reach the right person, let alone achieve results. It's worth spending a few minutes planning what you're going to say and making sure that you're speaking to the decision-maker before you launch into a conversation. Once you've built some rapport, you can ask questions to identify their needs before explaining how you're the best person to meet them. When you have a clear structure to follow, you're less likely to miss these important steps.

Another area in which it's helpful to be prepared is when your potential client raises a concern about working with you. This can fluster even the most experienced recruiter, but the secret to succeeding here is to have up your sleeve some ways of countering objections. One method is to ask a series of questions to fully understand what's worrying the client, so you can offer a solution. Another is to reassure them that their concerns are understandable but that other clients you've worked with have found them to be a non-issue once they started working with you. While not a solution for every kind of challenge, this can go a long way towards making you a ready recruiter.

When you have a client meeting, always prepare yourself by researching the business beforehand and, if you can, bringing with you some relevant CVs. These will demonstrate the quality of your candidates, so that even if they're not all spot on you'll be showing initiative. Also, doing your fact-finding on the client ahead of time means that you can have a list of questions to hand, which avoids that face-palm moment in the car afterwards when you realise you forgot to find out what their standard benefits are or when they want the candidate to start.

Helping your clients to be proactive is another way to make sure that you're always ready. Have you ever presented one of your regular customers with a salary survey or industry update at one of your meetings? Or how about an advance warning about what's happening in their sector? Through your research, which as a relevant recruiter you'll naturally have been undertaking, you may unearth some changes that will affect what kind of employees they want to bring in. That way both you and they are prepared, and you'll come across as informed and proactive as well.

Listening to those client responses will then enable you to talk about what is appropriate to sell the dream and close the deal.

– Specialist Consultant

Read through a job spec and imagine doing that job – really put yourself in that position. If I worked for that company, what would I do? What does my day look like? What kind of person am I? What skills am I using? Then you start to understand more about what the client wants.

– Divisional Manager

Build a solid candidate pipeline

Recruitment is a proactive business, and there's nothing that defines a recruiter as being ready more than having a consistently high–quality stream of candidates at their fingertips. When you receive that call from a client with an urgent vacancy, you want to be confident that you can say 'yes' without frantically digging through the pile of unregistered CVs that have built up in your inbox. What actions are you taking to source those job seekers? Are you visiting the places where they hang out on- and offline enough, to see who's looking for a move? Bear in mind that you don't need to limit yourself to active candidates – 80 per cent of the people REED placed last year were passive ones who'd submitted their CVs some time ago. Why were we so successful in gaining their interest? Because they were the job seekers who weren't being called up by all the other recruitment agencies that were focusing only on people actively looking for work.

The secret of my success would probably be to always have the best candidate. Even if you're not the best salesperson, if you constantly have an excellent standard of candidates, companies will always come back to you.

– Recruitment Manager

When a candidate approaches you, always take that call even if you think it might not be the best, because you never know when they might be offering you exactly what you want. People looking for work aren't always proficient at marketing themselves, so you need to extract the information from them. Not only should you establish whether they could do the job, but also if they'd be a good fit for your client's organisation – otherwise you're wasting everyone's time (not the most productive way to go about things). If it's a temporary role you're filling, you obviously need to establish if they have the relevant skills but also, less obviously, to measure how proactive and adaptable they are. Your aim should be for your client never to interview a temporary worker – they just want them to start straight away.

And finally, you can save yourself a lot of wasted effort if you create what one of our recruiters calls a 'triangle of happiness' for each booking. I'll let that person explain what this means:

> *The candidate has to be paid enough to feel like they're respected, but not so much that they don't think they have to work; the client has to be charged enough to feel they're paying for quality, but not so much that they think they're being taken advantage of; and the consultant has to make enough money from that booking to feel like it's worth their time, but not so much that they rest on their laurels.*

– Area Manager

Stay alert

Change creates opportunities, so a significant element of being ready is keeping your eyes and ears constantly open. It can be easy in the day-to-day rush of phone calls, emails and meetings to become lost in a labyrinth of tasks, but do yourself a favour and come up for air several times a day. What's happening in the news? It could be a company going into administration, flooding the market with desirable candidates who would suit one of your clients. Or you might discover a target client of yours is merging with another business. Redundancies can be an opportunity both to identify quality candidates and provide support to HR – who will recruit again in the future – either at that company or elsewhere.

One recruiter picked out a relevant news story and found that there was a business opportunity within that news.

– Senior Area Manager

Another aspect of being in tune with what's going on around you is to train yourself to read between the lines of what people say. I'm sure you've experienced the frustration of booking someone in for an interview, only to receive an email from them the night before it explaining that they've changed their mind. Was there anything in their manner or conversation that could have prepared you for that? Could you have asked them more questions? This involves putting yourself in their shoes so that you can have the best chance of predicting how they're going to behave, because what you might think of as an attractive role might not seem the same to them.

A lot of recruitment is about reading what people are going to do.

– Business Manager

To sum up

- *Being organised gives you the dual advantage of being able to take advantage of unexpected opportunities and to bounce back from difficulties.*

- *Consistency is a quality we all prize because we like to know what to expect, so try not to drop any unwelcome surprises on anyone.*

- *Winning and keeping quality clients involves planning and preparation.*

- *One of your selling points should always be having a great candidate pipeline, ready to fill a vacancy at a moment's notice.*

- *Scanning the horizon for sales opportunities and sniffing out potential problems are all in a day's work for a ready recruiter.*

Chapter 4
The Rapid Recruiter

It's no surprise that the rapid recruiter's spirit animal is a hare, which has very fast and nimble reactions, because targeted speed is the name of the game. When a client has a vacancy, they usually want it filled without delay – whether it's for a marketing director who will influence the direction of the business or an admin temp who's going to save the department from drowning in paperwork. It's the same with candidates. Once they've returned from an interview they're eager to know if they've been successful, and if there's any hold-up they might be tempted to accept an offer from someone else rather than risk losing everything. Let's not forget about you, too. Your level of urgency is dictated not only by how important it is to keep your clients and candidates happy, but by your desire to reach your targets for the month (netting you a decent bonus in the process).

Recruitment is a business in which speed is vital. Just because a client asks you to fill a position doesn't mean they're not asking other agencies at the same time (or will do if you don't give them what they want quickly enough). Sometimes it can feel like you're chasing your tail all the time, but – on a good day at least – the speed of the job is what makes it exciting. When you've placed your first candidate of the day before your colleagues have even finished their morning coffee, there's nothing to beat that feeling.

*Always be thinking ahead –
you don't want to
lose the business
to another
agency.*

– Recruitment Manager

How to be rapid

I don't know whether you can teach urgency – maybe it's just something with which you're born. But I do know that you can set yourself up for success by having passion and energy, and these will naturally make you work quickly. The planning skills you learned in the previous chapter will stand you in good stead here, because being speedy is about knowing what needs to be done and what could stand in your way of achieving it. But to keep going week after week also requires energy and enthusiasm, so you need to look after yourself both physically and mentally. Here's how you can become rapid at what you do.

Think before you speak

So much of being a rapid recruiter comes down to eliminating the things that will slow you down. Good old-fashioned communication skills are part of this.

First, when you receive a new request from a client, establish how urgent it is. As any recruiter will tell you, if they ask a client when the new person should start, 'ASAP' is always the response. But what do they really mean by that? On questioning, it might turn out that the current job holder has a three-month notice period, which means you have a bit of time. It's just that to the stressed-out manager who's received their resignation that morning, it feels like an emergency. So take the time to ask the right questions – that way you can prioritise your urgent action on the right jobs and avoid wasting energy by rushing to fill the ones that can wait.

Next, make sure you take down the job details in an efficient way. Don't just rely on the client emailing you a job specification: take it over the phone or in person as well – this shouldn't take more than 30 to 40 minutes. Many specifications aren't well written and don't tell you half of what you need to know, so you'll end up having to fill in the gaps by phone in any case. Your aim should be to receive the job details, source the candidates within a few hours, and send your client a shortlist of CVs and availability dates by the same time the next day.

You might frame it as not wanting to be intrusive, but you can easily flip that on its head and say that your candidates are chasing you, so you need that feedback from your client.

– Executive Consultant

In fact, the best recruiters discuss their suitable candidates on their first call with a client. If you're a consultant for temporary workers especially, you should aim to fill the role on the phone even if it's at 8am. If you don't, the next call your client makes will be to your competitor. Of course, for you to do this you need to be familiar enough with your candidate pool to be able to call people first thing with a booking, and to know who can travel in by when. The best permanent consultants take a leaf from their temp colleagues' books and aim to secure at least a couple of interviews on the spot. 'Are you at your desk now? Great – I'm emailing the CV over . . . got it? If you take a look at their most recent job you can see they've used the same software as you and are exactly what you're looking for. They're available for interview on Thursday or Friday this week – which day suits you best?' This not only gives you an advantage over any other consultancy, but it also means that you receive immediate feedback on your CVs and can adjust them accordingly if needed. Slow recruiters assume that they have until the end of the week to book interviews, so they put off calling their candidates. Try not to be that person.

As you're sending that email, the next thing your fingers are doing is calling their phone number to discuss candidates. You've gone out of your way to find them and you need to make sure that you're acting quickly because otherwise you're just a 'busy fool', finding people that look good for the role but by the time you get back to them are off the market.

– Business Manager

Also, communicate to your client how rapidly you're working. It's no use you breaking your back to fill their requirements if they don't know about it. If you know your candidate has other interviews elsewhere, it would be good to let your client know because it will concentrate their mind on making a decision. There's nothing like the prospect of losing out to a competitor to spur a hiring manager into action.

And finally, rapid communication with your candidates is key. You don't want them to be offered the job and keep you on hold while they play your client against another one, so press them for an urgent decision. Nor do you want them to have to chase you for feedback – not being able to get hold of their consultant is one of the main gripes candidates have with recruitment agencies. Create a space in your schedule to keep them up-to-date, and they'll see the pace you're working at and respond accordingly. If you're slow, they will be too.

Tell the client what you plan on doing before you're going to do it. If you've got three good candidates tell them you've got three people calling you back at lunchtime, and then after lunch call the client with the great news that those three people are in. Don't let them have it all at once. Whet their appetite, build them up, and it'll be much, much better.

– Area Manager

Whenever you speak to a candidate, ask when they could interview. If you present a candidate to a client with an interview time, you're cutting out three conversations and back-and-forth between the parties. Then it's done – that is my biggest speed tip!

– Head of Improvement

Be proactive

Everything you've learned about being organised and having high-level communication skills comes together here, because being proactive is the rapid recruiter's holy grail. The better you've come to know your clients' organisations, the more likely you are to predict when an urgent role will come up, leaving you in an excellent position to fill it. For instance, you may find out during a personal visit that someone's about to leave their post – what better time to suggest pulling together a new job spec?

Once your candidates have been interviewed, there's a danger that your client will take their time making a decision, leading you to lose that job seeker to another company or – even worse – another recruitment agency. You want them to say yes, and fast, because many candidates will switch from their first choice to an alternative offer if they haven't heard back within a week or two. But how to achieve that, when your phone calls go unanswered and the client's impossible to reach? The answer is to insert yourself into the interview itself. How about asking to sit in and take helpful notes, or assist in some way? If the session goes well, you can catch your client when their enthusiasm is at its peak and suggest that they offer your candidate the job before anyone else snares them. This is far more effective than waiting until

*Plant the seed
early for a
better harvest.*

– Area Manager

the next day, by which time they've had the chance to become distracted by all their other responsibilities. You can take this even further by asking for an open diary, in which you book five interviews and are trusted to put the right candidates in front of your client. Then, with your client's permission, sit in on the final interview of the day to review how they've gone and agree next steps.

Being proactive can also net you new work. If your client is a large company you might find that different recruitment agents supply different departments, presenting a golden opportunity to you as a rapid recruiter. Next time you pay a visit, why not ask for the name of the manager who runs an area you're not familiar with, then happen to drop by and let them know how you can help? That's the way to extend your influence from a small base – it's amazing how placing one candidate can open the door to countless new leads. Some of the best new opportunities can be from organisations with which you already work.

Prioritise

Your rule of thumb should be never to give a client or a candidate a reason to go anywhere else, so being clear on what's most important in your day is critical. This involves having a razor-sharp focus (and maybe an espresso to hand, too). Believe me, the day you miss

It's so easy to come in on a morning and have a chat or a bit of a catch up, but actually that's the part of the day before candidates go into work, so you need to get to them then.

– Talent Acquisition Specialist

out on a juicy placement because you could have acted quickly, but didn't, will be a day you regret for months.

Developing the skill of picking out the keywords in a CV while scanning it will stand you in good stead, as will that of matching a job specification to a CV in record time. You're looking to correlate the main two or three skills and experience requirements with what a candidate has. This involves working smart rather than hard, because it's easy to become distracted by all the little tasks that build up on your desk each day. Your job is to win in this tough, fast-moving market, and to prioritise sending out your candidates' details so that your clients can see you're rapid and respond accordingly. This can take a bit of confidence, but that's why you're charging your fee – because you deliver at speed.

Be prepared

As you'll have worked out by now, a rapid recruiter is always doing something. So how do they cope with this? They develop solid, trusting relationships with their clients that make acting quickly easy. Once you've delivered a great bunch of candidates a number of times, you can short-cut many of the preliminaries such as you having to get to know their corporate culture and them screening every CV. This enables you to sprint off the

Think of your recruiter brand as being like a shoe shop – are your shelves stacked with the right product?

– Recruitment Manager

starting block more speedily than your competitors. You can even ask for a 24-hour exclusivity window, with the promise that if they're not satisfied with the candidates you recommend within that time they can go elsewhere, but if they like what they see they'll stick with you. This will give you an added incentive to act without delay.

Likewise, when you have a ready hotlist of candidates with available start dates, that speeds you up. With temporary workers, if you're able to offer a candidate you've placed regularly before and with great feedback, you're onto a winner because you'll know they'll do well for you. It's a race to fill temporary jobs and the finishing window can come down to minutes.

Another way you can be prepared is to have a few ready-made ways of ending conversations up your sleeve. You could call them 'closing lines' – you know, the kind of phrases you can use to wrap things up and make sure everyone knows what they're doing next. The first type is assumptive, such as 'I'll schedule your interview for midday on Friday and look forward to your call afterwards to tell me how it went.' The second is when you provide a couple of different options, with the idea that the other person will choose one of them rather than 'no'. So, 'Would Tuesday or Wednesday be more convenient for an interview?' Or you can simply set out the next steps and ask if they agree. For example, 'Based on what we've talked about, the best plan is for me to send you five CVs to read by tomorrow. Is that okay?' As you can see, all these techniques are just as useful when attempting to close a sale as they are in speeding up your everyday conversations.

Don't rush it

Being rapid doesn't mean being slapdash, frenetic or inattentive to detail, because that won't win you any friends — at least in the long term. When you try to crowbar candidates into roles that don't fit them, nobody wins, because the likelihood is that they'll not last their probationary period and your commission will be similarly short-lived. Your relationship with your client is a partnership, and when you scramble through a placement the bond of trust is broken.

Don't try to put square pegs in round holes. You need to be speedy, but not at the expense of quality.

– Divisional Manager

This is especially the case when you have a role that's difficult to fill. Sometimes you have to accept that it's going to take longer than you'd like, but this is where both your communication skills and the quality of your relationships with your clients come in. If you're able to gain permission from your client to take some extra time, you'll deliver a better result than if you pass them a sub-par candidate for the sake of speed. You may find your client appreciates your honesty, because the last thing they want is to keep wading through CVs that aren't up to the mark. Sometimes being rapid means a series of targeted actions over time rather than in one go.

A rapid recruiter isn't like a machine gun, it's someone who understands when to be rapid and when to be urgent in a more methodical way.

– Area Manager

To sum up

- *Recruitment is a fast-moving business in which both clients and candidates want instant results: being organised saves time.*

- *Communicating clearly and effectively will speed up your work because you'll minimise misunderstandings and the number of phone calls and emails you have to make.*

- *Proactivity will speed you up in countless ways because you're thinking ahead and solving problems before they arise.*

- *Knowing what's most important and acting on it will give you the biggest bang for your buck.*

- *Being rapid isn't the same as rushing – sometimes less haste more speed is the way to go.*

Chapter 5
The Resilient Recruiter

J ust like our spirit animal for resilience, the tortoise, a recruiter needs to create their own safe shell so they can take a deep breath when they need to and carry on.

I paid a visit to one of our recruitment offices recently and asked everyone how they were getting on. All was good, but as I was about to leave one of the newer recruiters pulled me aside. After several weeks of interviews, she told me, she'd successfully placed a temporary worker for a difficult-to-fill maternity cover – and this was for a client she'd fought tooth and nail to win a few months earlier, bidding against two other agencies. Everyone was delighted when she filled the post, until the Friday before the temp was due to start when he called to deliver the news that he was ducking out due to personal issues. It was impossible to find a replacement to start on the same day, especially as the office was in a small town. 'I felt sick,' she said. 'I knew I had to ring my client to tell her and it was the most frightening call I've ever made. But I just had to accept that this kind of knock-back is part of the job. I knew my role was to put myself in my client's shoes and find someone else as quickly as I could.'

I'm sure this situation isn't new to you. How about this story from another recruiter? 'As a recruitment consultant you sometimes find out about redundancies before your clients do. One time I had a meeting with a client who I had a great relationship with, and only an hour beforehand I'd discovered he wasn't going to have a job in a month's time. That was a piece of information I'd have been glad to be without. What could I do? I was sworn to secrecy so I couldn't say anything to him. Other times I've talked to candidates who are in tears because they've gone from earning £60k to stacking shelves. I've had to give it everything to keep going sometimes.'

It can be tough when you're faced with scenarios like these, can't it? When I carried out the research for this book there were more comments on the topic of resilience than on any other. It seems that every recruiter struggles in this area, because candidates and clients can be both demanding and changeable. The fact that recruitment is a people business makes it especially tricky to keep your sanity at times – after all, when you're selling a physical product it can't just change its mind the day before it's due to go on sale or do a disappearing act on you all of a sudden. But clients and candidates can.

> *The hardest thing in recruitment, without a doubt, is that people have a mind of their own. You can have worked on a vacancy for weeks or tried to win a client for years, and eventually you find the right candidate and they say, 'I don't want it.' You know it's going to take a long time to win the client's trust again.*

– Area Manager

It's the same when you're recruiting a new client. You've called them 14 times in the past month, emailed them 10, and even dropped by to say hello – all to no avail. At what point do you throw in the towel? And how do you cope with being top of the sales league one month but at the bottom the next (it happens to everyone)?

The two recruiters I mentioned above both experienced emotional and practical challenges, but they also showed the hardy spirit that's so essential in this job. Recruitment is both fast-paced and unpredictable, which means that it places huge demands on its consultants. You have to be rapid enough to win the work, but also possess the patience of a saint when things don't go according to plan. This stop-start pattern can wear a recruiter down, which is why resilience is such a vital part of your mental toolkit. Patience is often what wins the day. It's worth it, though, because as one of the senior recruiters I talked to pointed out:

I'd employ someone who was resilient over someone with intelligence, sales ability, customer service, personality – you can forget it all if you're not resilient. Recruitment is resilience. It's not a case of 'I can't', it's a case of 'I will'.

– Divisional Manager

How to be resilient

It's easy to feel resilient when you've just received a welcome bonus or had a pat on the back from your favourite client for filling a difficult vacancy. But what about when your seventh call to a prospect has been ignored, a key customer demands a rebate on your last placement, or a candidate you could have bet your life on being reliable doesn't show up for an interview? How do you cope then? The answer is to keep doing the right things at the right times and in the right way, and you'll eventually achieve results. Let's look at what that means.

Develop some emotional elasticity

Learning the skill of bouncing back is essential in this game. You need to have what I call one of the three Gs of the essential mindset: grit (the other two are good and global). This is a combination of determination, patience and courage – qualities that it's necessary to possess in spades. The good news is that it becomes easier to have these the longer you've been in recruitment, because you come to learn that after every bad day there's a chance to have a better one. You can have a terrible month – you know, the kind when you don't manage to arrange a single client interview and your boss says you need to put five in the diary this week – and the next day receive

Recruitment is always going to be hard, but it's brilliant.

– Area Manager

The beautiful thing about recruitment is it can always be Day 1. Even if everything's gone wrong and you've had a really tough time, every placement's fallen through or a candidate's done something wholly unexpected, you can always have Day 1 the day after.

– Area Manager

a call with 20 vacancies from a local company creating a customer service team. This really happened to one of our consultants, and that day could be tomorrow.

With our business, although the individual tasks you carry out aren't necessarily that hard, putting them together successfully can be complicated. So, accepting that recruitment is a career you have to *learn* to be good at is helpful; you wouldn't expect to master the trombone in a week, and nor should you give yourself a hard time if it takes a while get on top of the basics of recruitment. In fact, putting excess pressure on yourself to be perfect is a recipe for losing momentum — it's far harder to persevere if you're constantly berating yourself for not matching up to an impossible ideal. If nothing else, it's a commonly known fact that the happier you are the more productive you'll be. And having a sense of humour helps. A consultant I spoke with during my research confessed that he'd split a hole in the crotch of his trousers by stumbling on the stairs on the way into a client meeting. He had to manoeuvre himself sideways to hide it, and spent the whole session wondering how on earth he was going to leave at the end without turning around. The only thing that kept him going was imagining what an entertaining after-dinner story it was going to be.

If you have a positive outlook, you'll also find it easier to come across as friendly and optimistic with your clients and candidates. Holding yourself back from throwing yourself into your work because you're worried about how things will turn out, means that you won't achieve the results you want. Even when you have a bad month, you should have the confidence to know you're putting the work in, and that if you keep doing it you'll strike gold sooner or later. The drive to recruit will always be in you, no matter what happens in or outside the office.

It's also okay to feel affected when a difficult situation arises – you're only human. Part of being resilient is acknowledging this rather than pretending you don't care, because that way you can deal with it and move on (over and over again). In other words, it's what's within you that counts – your own mindset is what will carry you through good times and bad. It's a tough job sometimes, and there will always be days when you wonder why you bothered to get out of bed, but when you take a request from a new client or place a candidate who has superb potential it can feel worthwhile. Just recall that feeling when you're let down yet again.

What you can do

Okay, so you understand that it's all about your mindset, but what can you *do* to become a resilient recruiter? Surely there's some action you can take?

You do have to become resilient over the years. There are times when you think good things aren't happening, but if you continue to put in the work, they will come around again.

– Senior Executive Consultant

Don't let some bad news ruin your day, tell yourself it's part and parcel of the job and carry on.

– Senior Consultant

For starters, never leave filling a booking until when it's convenient for you – do it now. Don't risk losing it to another agency, because there's nothing more demotivating than someone else swiping your hard-won prize. Also, keep being tenacious and calling those prospective clients and candidates every week. That way, when a client has a vacancy coming up, you'll be on their mental list of people to contact, and if a candidate is thinking of moving on you'll be their first port of call. If you don't do this, you might slowly sink into a pit of despondency in which you convince yourself that you'll never get anywhere, so what's the point?

It's about going back to basics. You could work from a well-qualified target list with a limited number of clients (this means that you need to know your market). It's important to understand what's important to each of those clients – is it a candidate shortage, an industry change or a lack of access to useful information? Then you can plan how and when to contact each target and be consistent. If it's a 12-week plan and you give up after three weeks, you'll never build anything significant. Respond to your clients if they give feedback and, if they don't, think of another way to engage them such as inviting them to an event or sending something in the post. Just keep on doing the simple things brilliantly and consistently, and you'll get there in the end.

If the activity's there, the results will come.

– Divisional Manager

Next, become curious as to why things might not be working for you. One of the recruiters I spoke to referred to Basil Fawlty thrashing his car with a branch when it wouldn't work. Hilarious though that was to watch, it was obviously no way to get what he wanted. If he'd just relaxed, taken a deep breath and asked himself if there was anything else he could do to start the car, he might have succeeded. There's always another way to approach a problem, but if you're stuck in a cycle of frustration and disappointment you'll never see it. Recruitment can be an infuriating business at times, so cut yourself some slack and get out of the office for a bit if it helps. Taking a short walk or having a coffee can free your mind, and before you know it you'll have thought of an idea that will help you take the next step. Accepting that some clients and candidates will let you down on occasion by not keeping their promises will give you a sense of perspective, which is a key element of resilience.

Most recruiters agree that the hardest slog is always in the first year, when you're learning to stick your neck out and pick up the phone to call potential clients, or to make judgements about candidates when you're not sure if you're on the right track. This is when it's helpful to revisit the goals you set yourself at the beginning (or to make some if you haven't already). How far are you towards achieving them? You may be surprised at the distance you've travelled since you first took ownership

Don't be frustrated, be fascinated.

– Divisional Manager

of your desk, and if so give yourself some kind of reward – it will be an instant boost. If you're not pleased with what you see, ask yourself if you were being unrealistic. Success never arrives instantly in this business – for example, it takes an average of 12 weeks to convert a client from being a target to being active on your books, and that's only the ones with whom you succeed.

Another way of looking at this is to decide to do something outside of your comfort zone every day, if for no other reason than to prove to yourself that you can do it. This is especially important if you're a new starter. How about challenging a 'no' from a potential client, or trying a new way of talking to someone to see if it works? Not only will you be showing yourself that you can be brave, you'll also be preventing yourself from falling into stale habits. Ask yourself (in a curious way, without berating yourself) at the end of every day, 'What did I do to make myself feel uncomfortable today?'

It also helps to learn what a 'win' really means and to appreciate each and every one. Filling a job or gaining a new client isn't the only kind of success you can have – if you focus only on the main attractions you'll lose sight of the sideshows. What leads to these successes? Making calls, arranging meetings, sourcing quality candidates – these are all part of the process. Recruitment can be a lot of fun and there's a huge advantage in working in a

Recruitment is like a fine wine – it gets better with age!

– Senior Business Manager

profession where there's never a dull moment, so respect the little things.

And finally, don't forget the support network you have both within and outside of the office. Take the example of when someone's put the phone down on you. What do you do? You could berate yourself for being a useless person, or you could turn to your colleague and tell them what's happened. They're guaranteed to have had the same experience and you'll feel better if you talk about it. A sympathetic ear and some advice will go a long way. Also, what about your activities outside of work? Do you have friends and family you can open up to, or hobbies you enjoy that will pick you up after a terrible day? It's important not to make recruitment the only thing in your life. And when the day is done, make sure you have enough sleep. Being well rested will help your memory, creativity, problem-solving capacity and ability to remain resilient.

Take a fresh look at how you recruit and manage your clients

After you've spent a few months chasing a client it's easy to fall into a certain way of thinking about them, which is that they have all the power and you have none. A resilient recruiter, however, realises that this isn't necessarily the case. When you appreciate the value of

When you have paid off your bills, treat yourself to something – have a hobby, have something to live for outside of work. If you purely do this job, go home, sleep, eat . . . my goodness! I couldn't think of anything worse.

– Specialist Consultant

your service, you won't see yourself as someone doffing their cap to their master but as a skilled professional who can help transform an organisation by delivering the best staff. Even if you don't know it yet, you're the equal of the client you want to win because they need you as much as you need them. Understanding this helps you to keep going because you'll feel confident that it's only a matter of time before they realise the same.

When it comes to approaching a prospect, the best way to think about it is that *this* call or visit will be the one that wins you the business. The same goes for existing clients, because they'll always have a need for more vacancies to be filled. Look beyond the usual reasons for a 'no', such as 'we don't have the budget' or 'we never use recruitment agencies'. Find out why not, by using the objection-handling techniques we talked about in Chapter 3. For instance, you might need to highlight what it would cost them to hire the wrong person, and how much time they'd spend doing it without your help – you have access to candidates they don't even know exist.

Revisit how you find and manage your candidates

Keeping going when you're struggling to find the right person to fill a vacancy can be the ultimate frustration, especially when you have a client who's champing at

The moment you feel like you have to ask that director, 'Please sir, can I have some more?' it puts them on a pedestal.

– Business Manager

*Just do not give up.
It took me one year to
convert a big client – I
did it (I think I drove the
financial director mad
with my calls, emails,
mailers, etc.) They spend
thousands of pounds
with us now.*

– Recruitment Manager

the bit to spend money on you solving their problem. However, to keep your search sharp, there's nothing like the thought of a competitor stealing a vacancy from under your nose because they had access to a better candidate than you. Use every sourcing technique in the book, and don't neglect the more out-of-the-way places where your potential recruits may be hiding. Imagine how you'd feel if the one who was offered the job via another agency was someone under your nose all along – especially if they were on your database (or worse, if you found them but assumed they weren't suitable).

Your resilient approach doesn't end once you've placed a candidate. There are ways of keeping in touch that have the potential to gain you repeat business, such as giving them a call to see how they're getting on and asking to speak to their manager once you've finished, or paying their manager a visit and asking if they have any more vacancies coming up. You could even try this:

Find greater reward in greater difficulty

The easiest client relationships aren't necessarily the best. That manager who always says 'yes' and who seems eager to please is often like that with everyone. Also, sometimes the most difficult situations are those that bring you the most reward, and this can be a huge comfort when times are tough. I'll let one recruiter give a brilliant example of this in their own words:

> *I have one client who I took about seven months to build up a relationship with. On one occasion he actually called me back and said, 'You've got one opportunity to present a financial controller to me. If you do that we'll have a relationship forever, and if you don't we won't.' Years later he was at my wedding and I was at his. Persistence beats resistance.*

– Area Manager

Every period we have a candidate of the month. We visit them to give them a gift and a certificate, and it's just an easy win. We get to see the different managers and say our hellos, which means candidates and clients constantly see our faces.

– Business Manager

To sum up

- Recruitment is a people business, and as such is never predictable or reliable.

- Combining the rapidity and patience you need to succeed is never easy, which is why you need resilience: developing grit and determination, and cultivating an optimistic attitude, are vital.

- So too are becoming curious, acting outside of your comfort zone, using your support network and valuing every win; remember that easy wins aren't always the most rewarding.

- You don't need to feel in thrall to your clients, either prospective or current, as long as you're offering an excellent service.

- Make sure you use every available avenue to find the best candidates.

Chapter 6
The Reflective Recruiter

Whenever you find yourself operating on autopilot, ask yourself how you can 'be more owl' – the reflective recruiter's wise spiritual guide who has an all-round view of a situation.

Recruiters are action-takers by nature. Making 20 phone calls and sending 30 emails before lunch is a pretty normal day, and that's not taking into account the frantic rush from interview to client meeting and back to interview – it's non-stop. But you wouldn't want it any other way, would you? I don't imagine you chose recruitment so you could spend your time contemplating the meaning of life. You see it as a job where you can do things well, and rightly so.

But there's a downside to this, which is that when you don't set aside time to reflect on all that activity, or to develop the habit of looking inwards rather than outwards at least for a while, you won't improve as quickly as you'd like. Recruiters should have the inner wisdom and reflective qualities of the owl. No recruiter is born a top performer – they become one by analysing what they do and how they do it, and changing their behaviour as a result.

I love the phrase 'Better Never Stops', a saying that the New Zealand rugby team, the All Blacks, swears by. The players' philosophy is to keep improving, and if that's the attitude of the most successful sports franchise in history it should also be true for recruiters. This is a mission one of my recruiters, who joined us as a graduate, has always sworn by. He proceeded to climb the ranks to managing director, so the mantra clearly served him well!

The best consultants learn what they're good at, how they come across to people, what clients respond well to, the nuances of communicating effectively, and the best ways of managing their emotions and energy. They make mistakes just like everyone else, but they learn from them, and that's when the magic happens. There's no substitute for self-knowledge in this game.

If you can analyse what you've done wrong and change it, and know that what you're putting in is what you're going to get out, that's what carries you through.

– Divisional Manager

How to be Reflective

Learning and improvement are very important, so it helps to see inward reflection as a regular part of your job. It can be liberating to discover something new about yourself. I'd encourage you to give this a go, and here are some tips on how to do it.

Be curious

Remember what it was like to be a kid, when even the kitchen cupboards were a goldmine of exciting possibilities? Being curious never stops being fun, we just forget about it as we grow older. The good news is that when we question what we take for granted, it's fascinating to see what comes up.

Curiosity is equally useful whether things have gone especially well or badly, because it helps you to improve. If you have a terrible day, instead of beating yourself up about it, how about sitting back and asking some reflective questions? In the same way, if four out of your five candidates have been invited to interview, why wasn't the fifth? I like to say that good enough is never good enough.

Give yourself permission to learn.

– Head of Improvement

I sent five CVs and got no interviews. I thought, hang on, I really listened to that brief, what happened? So I had an in-depth conversation with the line manager for the role about what was missing, what he was looking for, and getting into the detail . . . I sent three more CVs and one of them was the best she'd ever seen, and consequently that candidate got the job.

– Recruitment Consultant

If this recruiter had accepted the rejection at face value, they'd probably have gone home and slumped on the sofa all evening. It was far more constructive to approach the problem in the spirit of, 'I wonder what went wrong,' instead of wallowing in self-pity. You can also ask yourself some self-reflective questions to help you improve your overall performance. Good ones to try are: 'If I were to do that again, would I do it the same way? Did I give a bad experience to any of my clients, colleagues or candidates today? Was that situation stressful, and if so, why did I see it like that?' By carrying out this questioning you're increasing your level of emotional intelligence, which is key to becoming a more self-aware person with whom people find it easy to work.

In fact, this questioning approach will stand you in good stead in pretty much every scenario. How about asking your candidates out for coffee? This will give you the opportunity to pick their brains and build up a good relationship at the same time.

Some recruitment agencies carry out satisfaction surveys among both their clients and candidates to see how well they're serving them. If the candidate feedback shows that you're not returning calls quickly enough, and your clients say you're not sending relevant CVs, you know you have a problem. You could even ask how you rank compared to other recruitment consultants with whom

I've just started handling higher-level candidates in accountancy who are earning 100k plus, and suddenly there's a lot on their CVs that I don't understand. I think if you're open and honest with people and you ask them, 'What does this mean?' it helps.

– Senior Executive Consultant

they've worked. If you're not top of the list, ask them why, and when you have the answer make sure you improve in that area and demonstrate this whenever you speak with them.

Create good habits

Habits make or break our day because we spend so much time carrying them out. They're also stubborn creatures – so easy to form and yet so hard to stop. The trick is to create as many good ones as possible and to try not to fall into the bad ones. Which sounds simple, but because many of our habits are picked up unconsciously it can take some reflection to see where they've built up.

If you have a bad month, it's worth asking yourself what habitual activity may have contributed to it. Have you fallen into a routine of only emailing CVs instead of calling clients to talk them through, or of making snap judgements about candidates that turn out not to be correct? Think back on what you've done in the months that have gone well, such as having more meetings, making more visits and calls, and sending more mailers, and you'll likely see a difference in routine. This will help you to create a benchmark of what good work looks like, and if you're feeling analytical you can even work out, for instance, how many interviews you need to arrange in order to earn a certain amount of money.

One brilliant question to ask a client is, 'What would you want to see on a CV that would make you want to interview that person?' Asking that helps you tailor exactly who you're looking for.

– Executive Consultant

It's amazing how easy it is to fall into bad habits. Remind yourself about what you did well, and keep doing those things.

– Area Manager

A positive habit you can create for yourself is to set aside a few minutes of reflection time at the end of each day, either at your desk or on your journey home. Ask yourself what successes you've had and what you could do to improve next time. This is also an opportunity to write the following day's to-do list so you're ready to go when you come in the next morning – you're combining practical activity with winding down. Other options are to keep a journal or have an app on your phone to record ideas that come to you at random moments (like in the middle of the night).

There's one thing to bear in mind about habits, though. We have a saying at REED: *habit can be a glass ceiling*. Which means that having a routine is a good thing when it speeds you up, but when it stops you trying something new it becomes a limiting factor. How about varying the ways in which you approach clients, for instance? There are four main routes: phone calls, visits, emails and social media. If you mix them up a bit your prospects are less likely to feel bombarded because you'll be approaching them from different angles, and you'll never know which one they prefer until you try it.

Reflect with those around you

As Bill Gates said, 'We all need people who will give us feedback. That's how we improve.' If one of the

What I try to do is list three things that went well in that day or week. No matter how hard the day's been, always try to remember a positive outcome no matter how small that win is. Having a period of reflection really helps people put stuff in perspective.

– Business Manager

Consultants can fall into the habit of thinking it's all about the phone, or it's all about email. I'd use the analogy of 'what creates fire?'

– Senior Business Manager

world's richest and most successful entrepreneurs can acknowledge this, surely we should too. Fortunately you work in an environment in which learning from others is easy, because you have a ready-made pool of experienced and talented recruiters right beside you every day: your colleagues.

Do you listen to calls made around the office to help you generate ideas? Do you turn to the person sitting next to you when you're not sure how to do something, and just ask how they'd go about it? I'm not suggesting that you compare yourself too closely with everyone else, because each desk is different, but you can use the expertise around you. Many agencies have a weekly or monthly session in which everyone is invited to contribute their learnings. If yours doesn't (or even if it does), consider instituting a regular lunch or coffee meet-up at which you can share your results in a more informal way. At REED we have our own business school where recruiters go for group training courses – this creates a strong *esprit de corps*, which makes reflection and feedback-giving easy and fun.

And when you've picked up a hot tip from a top biller in your office, don't just think, 'Hmm, that sounds useful,' but use it in a way that works for you. 'Pinch with pride' can be your watchword – borrow the best ideas and add your own twist to them.

Listen to your boss! It might sound stupid but most managers have been doing the job for a long time, and they've probably been around long enough to have made some really stupid mistakes – at least I have. They probably do know what they're talking about.

– Area Manager

Have a mentor who's not your manager and who you feel you can talk to, because it's daunting sometimes to talk to your manager when you don't think things are going that great.

– Business Manager

Keep reflecting on the big picture

It can be easy to assume that reflective analysis is all about the nitty-gritty, such as the way you greet clients, the number of calls you make and your candidate screening process. But reviewing your progress can take a big-picture form too, and this can be more motivating. How about pinning your goals for the next month in front of your desk and ticking them off as you go along? The sense of achievement you'll gain from that is enormous. You can also use this kind of thinking when you measure year-on-year retention of clients. It's best not to wait until the end of the year, though: do it as you go along – by the time you've lost a customer it's too late to do the soul-searching. And what about candidate retention, too? This is important, especially in a temp market. Do your candidates return, and are they happy for you to put them forward for jobs again?

Recognise what you've learned

Being reflective is one of a recruiter's most effective tools in the battle for resilience. It really is okay to make mistakes (as long as they're not big ones), and many people in the business find it takes a year or two for things to click into place. Even then there's plenty more to learn, but knowing your value and recognising your achievements are vital parts of your job. It's so easy to take the highs for granted and only focus on the lows, but try not to fall into that trap. As two of the recruiters I met said:

As a manager, I take two business cards from each consultant at the start of the year. I get them to write one personal and one business objective on the back. It's a constant reminder in review periods to see how people are meeting those objectives. The smaller objectives throughout the year are keeping them in line with their bigger goals.

– Area Manager

Inevitably you're going to make a few mistakes when you start and as you go along. But we're not doctors, are we? We're not going to kill anyone if we make a mistake. What's the worst thing that could happen? They're going to tell you to do one and put the phone down.

– Recruitment Manager

To sum up

- *Being reflective doesn't come naturally to all recruiters, but it's an essential tool for continuous improvement.*

- *Allow yourself to be curious about what's going well and not so well – it can be fun and useful and at the very least you'll become more emotionally intelligent.*

- *Habits are the cornerstones of our day, so make sure you have good ones.*

- *Don't forget you have a team of people around you who can help you to improve.*

- *Reflecting on how far you've come can be incredibly motivating.*

Chapter 7
The Rewarded Recruiter

The ultimate recruiter's spirit guide is a bee, which collaborates with its colleagues over an extended period of time to produce its reward – golden honey.

Maybe I'm biased, but I find it hard to think of a more rewarding job than being a recruiter. You have the chance to change people's lives for the better, to earn the gratitude of your clients and candidates for bringing them together, and to be a respected professional in your community. It's an enriching career, made all the more special by the fact that you're working with people day in, day out. In fact, it's a vocation.

I love recruitment!

— Recruitment Consultant

There is, of course, the financial reward to take into account as well, because being a recruiter affords you the potential to earn a seriously large amount when you include your bonuses. Even better, your income is largely under your control. Running a desk is like managing your own business, with the revenue you generate for your consultancy being directly linked to the figure that pops into your bank account. Recruiting mixes autonomy with being a team player and the ability to earn sizeable compensation, and this combination is what many recruiters find motivating. It's no wonder that the image of a bee springs to mind: working hard, keeping busy, independently seeking out new opportunities and collaborating with colleagues to produce the ultimate reward.

But what does being a rewarded recruiter really mean, and how do you achieve it?

I don't know where else I could have earned so much money, or had a career that evolved and where I've had so many different jobs (regions, specialisms) as recruitment. If you're passionate and don't dismiss it as a sales job, it's absolutely a career you can do really well at.

– Divisional Manager

How to find Recruitment Rewarding

Both emotional rewards and financial ones are at the heart of this job: it's a combination of the two that can make the job so fulfilling.

The emotional reasons why recruiters love their job

Being a recruiter can be challenging, so it's pretty clear that you need to enjoy the rewards if you want to stay in the game. Money alone won't keep you going when your latest candidate has turned up to an accountancy interview wearing scruffy trainers, or one of your clients has failed to return your calls for the seventh time this week. So apart from the financial benefits, what did the recruiters I spoke with say was in it for them? Plenty, as it turns out.

It seems that the main thing that warms your heart, while you're standing on the chilly train platform on your way home, is remembering the people you helped that day. This is especially the case with the candidates you

It's lovely when someone says, 'Thank you very much for finding me my dream job.'

– Talent Acquisition Specialist

placed. They may have handed over their career dreams and ambitions to you, which is a wonderful feeling in itself even without the opportunity it gives you to build individual and lasting relationships. It's touching when someone puts their faith in you.

There's also a chance to practise true altruism. You'll no doubt have dealt with people who've been made redundant and who you've supported in their job search, as well as candidates who don't look like an obvious match for a role in terms of experience, but who have that special something. One of the recruiters I met had recently found a job for a man who'd escaped civil war in his own country. The double satisfaction that comes from matching and delighting both candidates and clients is hard to achieve through doing many other jobs – certainly not by selling loans or cars. And when you become respected as someone who is helpful and has integrity, it's the ultimate payback.

I've done sales jobs before where I was selling space in the backs of magazines. I just didn't see the point. I did recruitment because it was actually finding someone a job – and I don't see that as being a hippy, I see it as being human.

– Area Manager

I had a new starter who, in his first year, most people wouldn't have kept. He wasn't good, although he worked hard. I decided to help him and he's now my most successful consultant. I've got something from him that you cannot buy: I've got his loyalty, because I showed him my time and commitment and saw his potential.

– Area Manager

It can also be fun and reassuring to work with a great team, forging the close bond that can only develop when you support one another through tricky times. Most recruiters I've worked with have nothing but praise for their colleagues, and there's no doubt that it can be a comfort to let off steam with the only people who know what your job is really like. There's an equal (some would say greater) satisfaction to be gained from *leading* a team of recruiters, too – seeing them grow in confidence and skill is an experience to treasure.

And finally, how about the variety of a recruiter's role? You have the opportunity to meet clients in different organisations, each with their own way of working. There's also the chance to cross over to new specialisms or locations. Because every day is different you're exposed to a wide range of challenges which – when you meet them successfully – build your confidence and teach you how to forge long-lasting relationships. Whether you decide to stay in recruitment or move to another career, these skills and attributes are invaluable for life.

The financial rewards

No matter how much we love our jobs, we all want to be paid for them. In recruitment, your potential to earn a significant income is high, and greater than someone with the equivalent experience and qualifications would have in many other careers. When you first started in the business you might have heard your colleagues discussing their bonuses and wondered what all the fuss was about, but I'm sure that when you received your first significant commission you thought to yourself, 'I can do this too!'

One of the financial aspects of recruiting that many people find rewarding is the way it gives you control over your own destiny. A recruiter said she'd saved for her whole deposit on her house by working extra hard for one year, and pointed out that there were few other jobs in which she could have achieved this without having to manage a huge team or work her way up the ladder over years.

This job suits my personality because if it was commission only I'd panic about how to pay my mortgage. If it was flat salary, I'd turn up to work and do my job because of my work ethic. But here there's that happy medium – we can effectively control how much we earn.

– Executive Consultant

To achieve this financial security, though, involves negotiation. Make sure that you charge what you're worth, especially with roles that are difficult to fill – when you value your service you'll find it easier to stick to your guns. It's easy to stumble with this at first. One recruiter recounted that, when he first started, a colleague passed a client call to him saying it was from 'an accounts assistant or something'. In fact it was the managing director of the company with which he was dealing, who wanted to know how much he was going to be charged. 'I'm looking for 15 per cent,' the client said, and because the recruiter felt flustered he agreed to it on the spot. There's a lesson in there for us all.

The truth is that no one is motivated by money, but by what it can buy them. This could be security and peace of mind, a luxury holiday or kids' school fees. Have you ever found that, when you had a hunger to buy something that meant a lot to you, you suddenly seemed to work that bit more enthusiastically? A good trick when you want to increase your income is to decide what you'd spend it on and picture it either mentally or with a physical image – this could be of the item you want to buy or your family – whatever motivates you to earn a bonus. One clearly defined goal with a photo of it by your desk is worth a dozen vague ambitions.

You can also use money as a way of keeping positive day to day by treating yourself when you've done well. Going out for a meal, buying a pair of designer sunglasses or booking a spa session are all examples I was given by recruiters for how they like to spend their spare cash. These treats are strong drivers for using every opportunity to generate income, 'like you're trying to scrape the last drop of honey from the jar', as one put it.

Every time you get a pay cheque that's above your monthly bleed rate and above what you might want to save, go and spend that cash on something stupid! Because you really will enjoy spending the money, and it'll make you want to get a pay cheque like that again.

– Area Manager

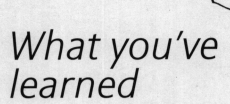

What you've learned

Here's a helpful checklist of learning points, drawing on everything you've read in this book. When you keep referring back to it over time, you create a virtuous circle – the more fulfilling you find your job and the more beneficial it is for people to work with you, the more rewarded you'll be in head, heart and bank balance.

- *Recruitment is a people business, with all the rewards and frustrations that brings. Being able to tap into your clients' and candidates' desires and fears, and to relate to them as individuals, are the cornerstones of your success. That's being **relatable**.*

- *Developing your knowledge as a specialist means that you can help people more effectively than if you were a generalist – it's as simple as that. And if you succeed in this area you'll earn the rewards. That's being **relevant**.*

- *Being organised and prepared may not seem exciting, but you'll earn dividends for your efforts when you have a constantly full candidate and client pipeline. That's being **ready**.*

- *Clients and candidates want fast results, so when you're proactive you'll not only be valued and respected by them but you'll also be likely to win a bonus as a result. That's being **rapid**.*

- *Some days will be good and some days will be bad. When you have a challenging day and manage to be curious about it instead of frustrated or downhearted, you'll be learning (and earning) more. That's being **resilient**.*

- *Because recruitment is one of those careers that never stands still, you have the chance to develop your knowledge about it forever. When you do this you'll be a truly professional recruiter. That's being **reflective**.*

- *Now all that remains for me to say is: learn, earn and succeed. That's being **rewarded**.*

People are everything in business and recruiters are right in the thick of it! I hope you enjoy your journey.

Acknowledgements

I would especially like to thank Ginny Carter, Imogen Burgess, Laura Holden, Roger Mason and Rosie Reed for doing the 'heavy lifting' for this book; I could not have completed it without you. I would also like to thank Rosie Reed for her beautiful animal illustrations as well as my agent, Robert Smith, my editor, Carey Smith and all the team at Ebury for their editorial input (Sam Crisp, Assistant Editor, has done a lot of work behind the scenes).

As I mentioned in *What Makes a Successful Recruiter?*, the research that was conducted to create this book was crowdsourced, and it would not have been possible without the help and contributions from everyone listed below. I am very grateful. Thank you.

Lucie Acellam, Lorraine Adams, Eleanor Ashley, Chelsea Atherton, Matt Atkinson, Lisa Avenell, Amy Avery, Husam Awadalla, David Baker, Richard Barker, Emma Barnes, Helen Barrett, John Barron, Kate Barros, David Bass, Amanda Beeson, April Bestford, Karen Birch, Rebecca Blankenbyl, Sam Boden, Steve Botting, Milly

Bourke, Shaun Bourke, Judy Bourouf, Stephen Brauner, Stephanie Brennan, Emma Briers, Laura Briggs, Robin Broster, Lucy Buckland, Catherine Bunting, Niall Burton, Mike Butler, Alex Byrne, Nick Callaghan, Alexia Catt, Paul Caudell, Ryan Claire, Jim Clarke, Phil Clarke, Joanna Clarkson, Mary-Anne Clayton, David Constance, Toni Cook, Amber Coplad, Rosie Corney, Andy Cox, Andrew Cranna, Surinder Curry, Dallas Dacre Lacy, Claire Davis, Jon D'Costa, Carmen De Jager, Pat Deeley, Richard DeNetto, Simone Devereux, Greg Divall, Mathew Dodd, Mike Duggan, Natasha Dwyer, James Eastwood, Charlie Elgar, Caroline Ellis, Kevin Elvin, Alex Farbon, Stephen Farquhar, Henry Field, Tony Finn-Ford, Hazel Flanagan, Jo Fornaciari, Amy Foster, Daniel Foster, Sian Franklin, Ben Fuller, Jean-Pierre Gadsdon, Richard Garbett, Mike Gardner, Nicole Gardner, Andrew Glass, Dominic Gold, David Gordon, Richard Gould, Pippa Graham, Marcus Granville, Alex Green, Beth Green, Jayne Green, Julie Gregson, Jacquie Griffey, Kate Groves, Daniel Gualdino, Nichola Gudger, Stacey Hartman, Matt Heather, Austin Heraty, Joe Hind, Mel Hinde, Sarah Hindmarsh, Jim Hoare, Jan Hogger, Peter Holmes, Wayne Hope, Emma Houghton, Stephanie Houghton, Will House, Adele Houston, Sarah Howard, Jac Humphreys, Philip Isaacs, Abdul Jaffer, Laura James, Zoe Jarrold, Oliver Jennings, Lisa Johnstone, Michael Jones, Lee Jones, Rohan Kallicharan, Gordon Kaylor,

Mark Keeler, Ruth Keeper, Mark Keizner, Sarah Kemp, Rona Khatun, Joanne King, Sian Lacey, Jessica Larner, Alison Lees, Rebecca Leggatt, Nick Legge, Matthew Lema, Paul Lenzan, Catherine Leonard, Margaret Levett, Annabeth Limb, Rebecca Lines, Francesca Lloyd, Tom Lovell, James Lucas, Holly Lyall, Natasha Mackness, Shada Mahboob, Connor Mason, Martin May, Leigh McComish, Catherine McCormack, Lucy McDermott, Hilda McManus, Ita Mcneil-Jones, Emma Meen, Antonio Miragliotta, Molly Mitchell, Isobel Morgan, Simon Morris, Jon Moss, Laurence Nash, Ian Nicholas, Alex Nicholls, Daniel Noble, Michelle Northcott, Vicky O'Brien, Jeanette O'Connell, Jeanette O'Connell, Victoria O'Connor, Katt O'Donnell, Dave O'Keefe, Jennifer Otoo, Francesco Pasqualitto, Eleanor Patel, Richard Paxton, Lizzie Peck, David Pennell, Rhys Penny, Lisa Percival, Steve Philcox, Joanie Player, Duncan Pleass, Magda Ploch, Claire Plume, Timothy Pool, Carrie-Anne Porter, Dave Poulter, Oliver Povey, Alexandra Powell, Carla Powell, Wendy Preedy, Gary Pugh, Bev Pullin, Jamie Rafferty, Paul Raggett, Kelly Randall, Andrea Raven-Hill, Becky Read, Mei Reddaway, Nicola Reed, Sir Alec Reed, Kurt Reed, Andy Reeves, Jo Remizova, Mark Rhodes, Paul Ridley, Neil Roberts, Ben Roberts, Ed Robinson, Emma Rogers, Julie Rose, Mark Rose, Lavina Rose, Elizabeth Rowe, Carol Rowson, Gurjit Ruprah, Rachel Saunders, Alan Scott,

Janet Scott, Ardil Shaikh, David Shaw, Jody Shepherd, Tim Shepherd, Amanda Shoyer, Deborah Sibley, Kerry Simms, Stewart Smith, Andrew Snell, James Soden, Claire Spiteri, Catherine Squibb, Lisa Stairs, Will Stanley, Dee Stead, David Stimson, Gary Strong, Kelly Strong, Hemal Tailor, Greg Taylor, Daniel Telfer, Neil Thomas, Sean Tomey, Charlie Underwood, Pam Underwood, Matthew Venables, Sue Walker, Kate Waller, Michael Ward, Michelle Ward, Charlie Wheeler, Georgia White, Kate White, Stephanie White, Ken Wilkins, Caroline Wilkinson, Claire Williams, Olivia Williams, David Wilson, Kerry Woods, Michelle Wright, Jo Wynsor, Josephine Youssefi, Chris Zammit.

There are many others that I have spent time with and spoken with over the last 25 years who have made an indelible impression and whose inputs and ideas are enduring. You know who you are. Thank you.

I feel hugely grateful to have worked with such outstanding people for such a long time.
Thank you all.

About the Author

James Reed has been recruiting for more than 25 years and is the Chairman and Chief Executive of REED, Britain's biggest and best-known recruitment brand and the largest family-owned recruitment company in the world. Since James joined the company in 1992, REED has grown into a billion-pound business and reed.co.uk has become one of the leading job sites in the UK and Europe. The business receives more than 40 million job applications a year, and has delivered over 100 programmes to help more than 150,000 long-term unemployed people back into work. It's now a global recruitment firm, with more than 3,500 people working in 140 locations around the world.

In 2018 James was voted Top CEO by employer-ratings platform Glassdoor, and in 2019 REED won a coveted Best Places to Work award from the same company. That means it's the top-ranked recruitment company on the list of all organisations voted as excellent workplaces by employees on Glassdoor.

A Fellow of the Chartered Institute of Personnel and Development, James is also the author of three bestselling books: *Why You? 101 Interview Questions You'll Never Fear Again; Put Your Mindset to Work*; and *The 7-Second CV: How to Land the Interview*, which was published early in 2019.

Index